بِسۡمِ اللهِ الرَّحۡمٰنِ الرَّحِيۡمِ

In the name of Allah,
the
Beneficent, the Merciful

RECONCILING THE RELIGIONS OF MOSES, JESUS AND MOHAMMAD (PBUT)

zulfikar H. Shah

Dedicated to my late father, Iqbal H. Shah, who was a kind, generous and helpful gentleman. And to the world, with prayers of peace and prosperity

Special thanks to my daughter, Salam Syed, for helping me with this project

بِسْمِ اللهِ الرَّحْمٰنِ الرَّحِيْمِ

In the name of Allah,
the Beneficent, the Merciful

Contents

Note from the Author

There is dire ignorance and misunderstanding on both sides – that of the Muslims as well as the People of the Book. This very fact created among them and caused conflicts, terrorism and wars. It destroyed millions of lives, wealth of nations and human dignity. It plundered the countries and slaughtered human beings on a massive scale. I am not

a writer or thinker by
profession, still I have
been highly compelled by our
global events. For quite
some time I had been
comtemplating how to do
something in my means to
help stop this ideology of
hatred, intolerance and
destruction.
For many years my soul has
been depressed. Many years I
have thought, delved, read
and researched to find the
truth. I am writing this
book very honestly,

impartially, diligently for
the common people and the
people of power to help them
understand the philosophy
and teachings of divine
religions. It will help us
understand, who we are,
where we came from and how
we are related to one
another. Are we friends,
foes or relatives of one
another?
Lastly, only those people
can benefit from this book
who are willing to bury the
hatchet, arrogance, greed,

ignorance and superiority complex. Those who want to explore the truth and educate themselves. People who wants to enjoy the fruits of peace and prosperity, who seek the pleasure of their creator and love to be successful in this world and in the hereafter.

May God accept my prayers and efforts.

Sincerely,

Zulfikar Shah

I. Hierarchy of the Prophets

The three prophets of God:
Moses, Jesus and Mohammad
(pbut) are the most
distinguished and have
billions of followers, even
today. They were bestowed
upon with divine books for
the guidance of humanity.
Each of these three great
personalities are holy
prophets and messengers of
God, who were sent upon
humanity in different times.
Many more prophets came
before them – some with

other books, depending on
the time.

Allah tells us in the Quran
about the following books:

- The Suhuf (Scriptures)
  were revealed to Prophet
  Ibrahim/ Abraham (pbuh)

- The Tawrat (Torah) was
  revealed to Prophet
  Musa/ Moses (pbuh)

- The Zaboor (Psalms) was
  revealed to Prophet
  Dawud/ David (pbuh)

- The Injil (Bible) was revealed to Prophet Isa/ Jesus (pbuh)

- The Qur'an was revealed to Prophet Mohammad/ Ahmed (pbuh).

Prophets Moses, Jesus and Mohammad are considered founders of Judaism, Christianity and Islam, respectively, based upon their teachings and books. The followers of each of these religions are referred

to as Jewish, Christians,
and Muslims, respectively.
Chronologically, Judaism is
more than 3000 years old,
Christianity is over 2000
years old religion and Islam
goes back about 1500 years.
Historically, all these
religions are Abrahamic
religions because they can
be traced back to the Holy
Prophet Abraham and his
teachings. Not only are the
religions sequential, the
prophets also have a shared
ancestry.

See the ancestry and family
tree of the Prophet Abraham
below:

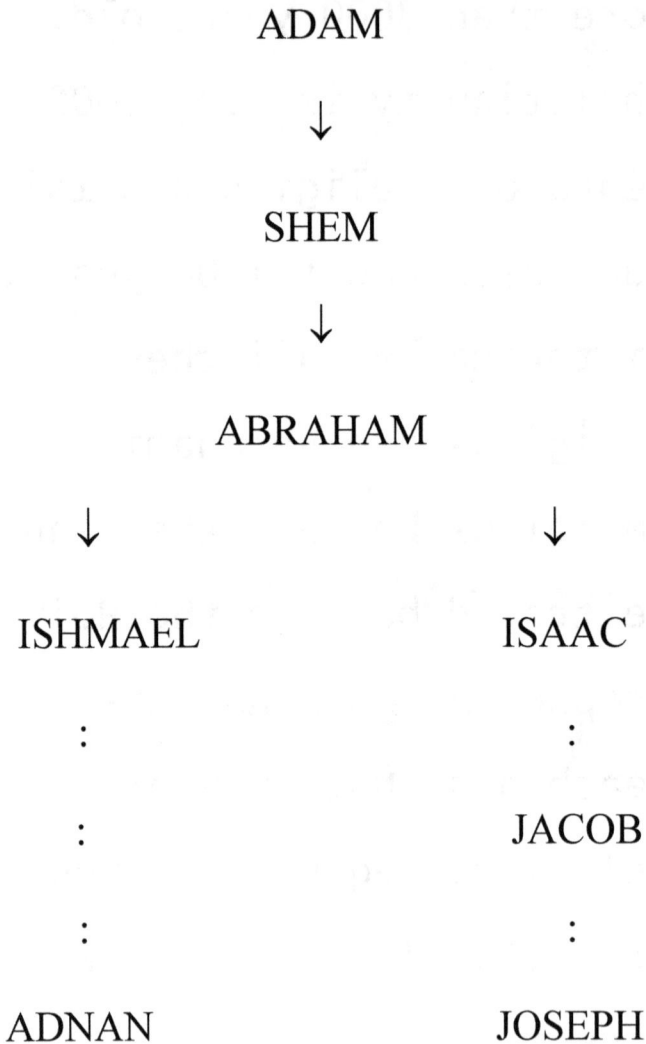

ADAM

↓

SHEM

↓

ABRAHAM

↓	↓
ISHMAEL	ISAAC
:	:
:	JACOB
:	:
ADNAN	JOSEPH

                    :   MOSES

                    :   :

                                                       DAVID

                    :   :

                                                 JESUS CHRIST

        MOHAMMAD

A detailed

genealogy of the Prophets:

Salasilah Nabi/Rasul

Direct descendant
Skip generation(s)

Adam — Sheth — Anwas — Qinan — Mahlavil — Yarid — Idris — Mahlabil — Lamik

Nuh — Sam / Ham / Yafid

Arfakhshad — Shalikh — Abir — Falikh — Ra'u — Saru'

Iram — Samud — Abir — Aus — Salih

Hadsir — Ibrahim — Ismail — Aziz — Nafur

Ash — Hadhir — Auf — Masir — Itbayd

Awih / Ad / Khulud / Raya / Abrahilah / Hud / Haran / Lut

Marayyan

Ishaq — Ya'qub

Isy — Rum — Tareikh — Amose — Ayyub — Zulkifli

Yahudza — Perez — Hasrun — Raum — Ummanizab — Yauksun — Salmun — Yuar — Ufiz — Isya

Yusuf / Bunyamin / Alhumfra / Matta / Yunus

Levi — Kohath — Imran — Harun — Izar — Fahraz — Yasin

Musa — Uhtub — Alyasa' — Ilyas

Satiyun — Syu'ib

'Uwaid — Isya / Thayut — Sulaiman — Hezekion — Hali / Maryam — Isa

Zakaria — Yahya

Qusai — Abd Muraf — Hashir — Abdul Mutalib — Abdullah — Muhammad

Fahr — Ghalib — Lo'i — Ka'b — Murrs — Kilab

Filas — Mudrikah — Khuzza man — Kinana — An-Nadir — Malik

Hunaise' — Add — Adnan — Me'ad — N zar — Mudar

Qawwam — Obai — Qamwol — Buz — Awis — Salaman

Jah.ir — Tabikh — Yadfad — Bidaa — Hoza — Nashid

Aram — 'Azhra / Sami / Mukasar / Alham / Desthan / Aid / Yahtin

Wuzzi / Zarih / Hiarith / Aftaad / Aktar / Ar'awi / Yalfean / Santir / Yalfeabi / Ad-Da'a / 'I thint / Malhi / Naifeah

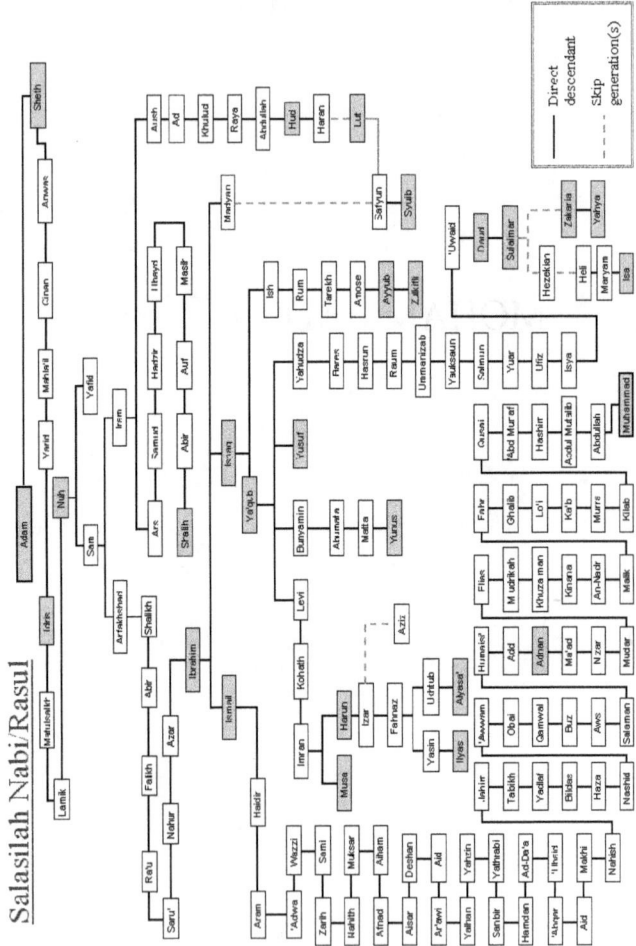

As these diagrams show, all
the prophets of God have a

common ancestry. Moses (pbuh), Jesus (pbuh), and Mohammad (pbuh) can be traced back to Prophet Abraham (pbuh), with Mohammad (pbuh) as the last prophet in this chain.

In Surah 33, Al-Ahzab, verse 40 of Quran, God promulgates:

مَا كَانَ مُحَمَّدٌ أَبَآ أَحَدٍ مِّن رِّجَالِكُمْ وَلَٰكِن رَّسُولَ اللَّهِ وَخَاتَمَ النَّبِيِّنَ ۗ وَكَانَ اللَّهُ بِكُلِّ شَىْءٍ عَلِيمًا ﴿٤٠﴾

"Muhammad not a father of any of your men, but a

messenger of Allah and the last of the prophets. And, Allah has the knowledge of everything."

Again in Surah 7, verse 158 of the Holy Quran, God declares the appointment of His Prophet.

سُوْرَةُ الْأَعْرَاف

قُلْ يَاَيُّهَا النَّاسُ اِنِّى رَسُوْلُ اللهِ اِلَيْكُمْ جَمِيْعاً الَّذِىْ لَهُ مُلْكُ السَّمٰوٰتِ وَالْاَرْضِ لَا اِلٰهَ اِلَّا هُوَ يُحْىٖ وَيُمِيْتُ فَاٰمِنُوْا بِاللهِ وَرَسُوْلِهِ النَّبِىِّ الْاُمِّىِّ الَّذِىْ يُؤْمِنُ بِاللهِ وَكَلِمٰتِهٖ وَاتَّبِعُوْهُ لَعَلَّكُمْ تَهْتَدُوْنَ ﴿١٥٨﴾

32

"O men! I am sent unto you all, as the Messenger of Allah, to whom belongeth the dominion of the heavens and the earth: there is no god but He: it is He that giveth both life and death. So believe in Allah and His Messenger, the unlettered Prophet, who believed in Allah and His words: follow him that (so) ye may be guided."

II. SUCCESSION OF THE PROPHETS & THEIR BOOKS

The Torah, revealed through Prophet Moses, is mainly about divine laws and regulations for the people of that time. The Book of Prophet David, the Zaboor, holds details about worship of God, including information about prayers, asking for forgiveness, etc. Next, there is the Bible, the Book of Prophet Jesus, which contains philosophy and elaborations of the Torah and Psalms. It describes the rationale of

the religion and its spirit.
Finally, there is the Quran,
the book that was revealed
onto Prophet Mohammad, which
builds upon the revelations
of each of the prior books.
It describes the mission of
the prophet of God and the
dialogue of the Messenger
with his people. It also
describes the laws, prayers
and philosophy of Islam.

Despite the large gaps of
time between the revelations
of each of these books, the

core values and fundamental principles of all these religions are the same. Some specific rituals and laws have been revised or introduced in the final book of God, the Quran, to tailor to the evolution of mankind.

To prove this fact of common core values and rules in the divine Religions, let us do a little research and navigate the famous Ten Commandments of the Old

Testament and the New Testament in the Quran.

The 10 Commandments List

1. YOU SHALL HAVE NO OTHER GODS BEFORE ME.
2. YOU SHALL NOT MAKE IDOLS.
3. YOU SHALL NOT TAKE THE NAME OF THE **LORD** YOUR GOD IN VAIN.
4. REMEMBER THE SABBATH DAY, TO KEEP IT HOLY.
5. HONOR YOUR FATHER AND YOUR MOTHER.
6. YOU SHALL NOT MURDER.
7. YOU SHALL NOT COMMIT ADULTERY.
8. YOU SHALL NOT STEAL.

9. YOU SHALL NOT BEAR FALSE
WITNESS AGAINST YOUR NEIGHBOR.
10. YOU SHALL NOT COVET.

Quranic version of the Ten Commandments can be found in chapter 17 surah Al- Isra / Bani Israel. They are presented below, in the order they appear in the Quran.

(Ist commandment)

لَا تَجْعَلْ مَعَ اللهِ اِلٰهًا اٰخَرَ فَتَقْعُدَ مَذْمُوْمًا مَّخْذُوْلًا ﴿٢٢﴾

Do not set up any other god along with Allah, otherwise

*you will sit condemned,
forsaken. (22)*

(2nd + 5th Commandment)

وَقَضَىٰ رَبُّكَ أَلَّا تَعْبُدُوٓا۟ إِلَّآ إِيَّاهُ وَبِالْوَالِدَيْنِ إِحْسَانًا ۚ إِمَّا

يَبْلُغَنَّ عِندَكَ الْكِبَرَ أَحَدُهُمَآ أَوْ كِلَاهُمَا فَلَا تَقُل لَّهُمَآ

أُفٍّ وَلَا تَنْهَرْهُمَا وَقُل لَّهُمَا قَوْلًا كَرِيمًا ﴿٢٣﴾

*And your Lord has decreed
that you worship none but
Him. And that you be dutiful
to your parents. If one of
them or both of them attain
old age in your life, say
not to them a word of
disrespect, nor shout at
them but address them in
terms of honour. (23)*

(3rd Commandment)

وَاٰتِ ذَا الْقُرْبٰى حَقَّهٗ وَالْمِسْكِيْنَ وَابْنَ السَّبِيْلِ وَلَا تُبَذِّرْ

تَبْذِيْرًا ﴿٢٦﴾

*And render to the kindred
their due rights, as (also)
to those in want and to the
wayfarer: but squander not
(your wealth) in the manner
of a spendthrift. (26)*

(6th Commandment)

وَلَا تَقْتُلُوْۤا اَوْلَادَكُمْ خَشْيَةَ اِمْلَاقٍ نَحْنُ نَرْزُقُهُمْ

وَاِيَّاكُمْ اِنَّ قَتْلَهُمْ كَانَ خِطْأً كَبِيْرًا ﴿٣١﴾

*And kill not your children
for fear of poverty. We*

42

shall provide for them as well as for you. Surely, the killing of them is a great sin. (31)

(7th Commandment)

وَلَا تَقْرَبُوا الزِّنَى إِنَّهُ كَانَ فَاحِشَةً ۖ وَسَآءَ سَبِيلًا ﴿٣٢﴾

Nor come nigh to adultery: for it is a shameful (deed) and an evil, opening the road (to other evils). (32)

(6th Commandment)

وَلَا تَقْتُلُوا النَّفْسَ الَّتِي حَرَّمَ اللهُ إِلَّا بِالْحَقِّ ۗ وَمَن قُتِلَ

مَظْلُومًا فَقَدْ جَعَلْنَا لِوَلِيِّهِ سُلْطَانًا فَلَا يُسْرِف فِّي الْقَتْلِ ۗ

إِنَّهُ كَانَ مَنْصُورًا ﴿٣٣﴾

Nor take life which Allah has made sacred— except for just cause. And if anyone is slain wrongfully we have given his heir authority (to demand Qisas or to forgive): but let him not exceed bounds in the matter of taking life: for he is helped (by the Law). (33)

(10th Commandment)

وَلَا تَقْرَبُوا مَالَ الْيَتِيمِ اِلَّا بِالَّتِي هِيَ اَحْسَنُ حَتّٰى يَبْلُغَ اَشُدَّهٗ ۖ وَاَوْفُوا بِالْعَهْدِ اِنَّ الْعَهْدَ كَانَ مَسْـُٔوْلًا ۞٣٤۞

Come not nigh to the orphan's property except to improve it until he attains the age of full strength; and fulfil (every) engagement, for (every) engagement will be enquired into (on the Day of Reckoning). (34)

(8th Commandment)

وَاَوْفُوا الْكَيْلَ اِذَا كِلْتُمْ وَزِنُوْا بِالْقِسْطَاسِ الْمُسْتَقِيْمِ ۚ ذٰلِكَ خَيْرٌ وَّاَحْسَنُ تَأْوِيْلًا ۞٣٥۞

And give full measure when you measure, and weigh with a straight balance. That is fair, and better at the end. (35)

(9th Commandment)

وَلَا تَقْفُ مَا لَيْسَ لَكَ بِهِ عِلْمٌ ۚ إِنَّ السَّمْعَ وَالْبَصَرَ

وَالْفُؤَادَ كُلُّ أُولَٰئِكَ كَانَ عَنْهُ مَسْئُولًا ﴿٣٦﴾

And follow not (O man i.e., say not, or do not or witness not) that of which you have no knowledge. Verily! The hearing, and the sight, and the heart, of each of those one will be questioned (by Allâh). (36)

The 4th commandment that says holy day is Sabbath day. It is Saturday for Jewish peoples and Sunday for Christians. In Quran there is relating verse in Surah Jumma which declares a holy day of the week for Muslims. Though it is not Saturday or Sunday, instead it is Friday.

Now, these questions arise: which religion is the right religion? And, which book are we to follow?

Surprisingly to many, all of the aforementioned religions are right since these are all books of God. Human misunderstanding, ignorance, personal biases and pride, in addition to our relationship with our time and geography, causes conflicts and disputes. Otherwise, all these books are commandments of God, carrying the same core values, rules, and regulations. They all endorse and support one another. They are the messages of the same God, sent to the mankind to follow throughout history via his splendid Prophets. Although revealed to particular nations, these messages were meant as guidance for all human beings of the time to follow.

The discrepancies in the religions, then, are a result of their chronological order.

Consider Microsoft Windows as an analogy for religion. As there are several versions of Microsoft Windows present today, such as Windows XP, Windows Vista, Windows 7 and Windows 8, there are various versions of the true religion. Each is a modified and improved version of the preceding one. The difference would be that although newer versions of Microsoft Windows continue to arise, there will be no more modifications to the true religion. The Quran is the final book and the Prophet Mohammad (saw) is the last Prophet of God.

The following verse was revealed to the Prophet Mohammad (pbuh), after he delivered his last historical Sermon in the vast ground of Arafat, when he performed his first and last

Hajj. It highlights that Islam is the perfected version of the religion.

In Surah 5, verse 3 God declares:

حُرِّمَتْ عَلَيْكُمُ الْمَيْتَةُ وَالدَّمُ وَلَحْمُ الْخِنْزِيرِ وَمَآ

أُهِلَّ لِغَيْرِ اللّٰهِ بِهِ وَالْمُنْخَنِقَةُ وَالْمَوْقُوذَةُ وَالْمُتَرَدِّيَةُ

وَالنَّطِيحَةُ وَمَآ أَكَلَ السَّبُعُ إِلَّا مَا ذَكَّيْتُمْ ۚ وَمَا ذُبِحَ عَلَى

النُّصُبِ وَأَنْ تَسْتَقْسِمُوا بِالْأَزْلَامِ ۚ ذٰلِكُمْ فِسْقٌ ۗ أَلْيَوْمَ

يَئِسَ الَّذِينَ كَفَرُوا مِنْ دِينِكُمْ فَلَا تَخْشَوْهُمْ

وَاخْشَوْنِ ۚ أَلْيَوْمَ أَكْمَلْتُ لَكُمْ دِينَكُمْ وَأَتْمَمْتُ

عَلَيْكُمْ نِعْمَتِي وَرَضِيتُ لَكُمُ الْإِسْلَامَ دِينًا ۚ فَمَنِ

اضْطُرَّ فِي مَخْمَصَةٍ غَيْرَ مُتَجَانِفٍ لِإِثْمٍ ۙ فَإِنَّ اللّٰهَ غَفُورٌ

رَّحِيمٌ ﴿٣﴾

"Today those who disbelieve
have lost all hope of
(damaging) your faith. So,
do not fear them, and fear

me. Today, I have perfected your religion for you, and have completed my blessing upon you, and chosen Islam as Deen (religion and a way of life) for you"

~

The next issue is to understand the need for so many prophets and holy books, instead of just one of each. To understand the difference among the prophets of God, let's compare them to Ambassadors of a sovereign country. Prophets are the Ambassadors of the kingdom of God sent from time to time to all the human beings alive at that time. The main difference is that Ambassadors are sent to a particular country, whereas Prophets were sent to the whole mankind of that time. Because the whole world is the kingdom of one God. All the prophets are equally virtuous and respectable - there is no difference, whatsoever, amongst them.

Surah Al-Baqarah/The Cow, verse 285 says:

أَمَنَ الرَّسُوۡلُ بِمَاۤ أُنۡزِلَ اِلَيۡهِ مِنۡ رَّبِّهٖ وَ الۡمُؤۡمِنُوۡنَ ۚ كُلٌّ اٰمَنَ بِاللّٰهِ وَمَلٰٓئِكَتِهٖ وَكُتُبِهٖ وَرُسُلِهٖ ۚ لَا نُفَرِّقُ بَيۡنَ اَحَدٍ مِّنۡ رُّسُلِهٖ ۚ وَقَالُوۡا سَمِعۡنَا وَاَطَعۡنَا ۖ غُفۡرَانَكَ رَبَّنَا وَاِلَيۡكَ الۡمَصِيۡرُ ۞٢٨٥

"Believe in God, His Angels and His books and His Prophets, Do not make any distinction / discrimination among any of the Prophets."

Now the question arises, why God (Allah) bestowed three different divine Books upon these three Prophets. Why did he not just reveal one

56

final version of the Divine
Book to be followed by all.
Its answer is right in Al-
Quran, Surah 5, verse 48:

وَأَنْزَلْنَا إِلَيْكَ الْكِتَابَ بِالْحَقِّ مُصَدِّقًا لِّمَا بَيْنَ يَدَيْهِ

مِنَ الْكِتَابِ وَمُهَيْمِنًا عَلَيْهِ فَاحْكُمْ بَيْنَهُمْ بِمَا أَنْزَلَ

اللَّهُ وَلَا تَتَّبِعْ أَهْوَاءَهُمْ عَمَّا جَاءَكَ مِنَ الْحَقِّ لِكُلٍّ

جَعَلْنَا مِنْكُمْ شِرْعَةً وَّمِنْهَاجًا وَلَوْ شَاءَ اللَّهُ لَجَعَلَكُمْ

أُمَّةً وَّاحِدَةً وَّلَكِنْ لِّيَبْلُوَكُمْ فِي مَا آتَاكُمْ فَاسْتَبِقُوا

الْخَيْرَاتِ إِلَى اللَّهِ مَرْجِعُكُمْ جَمِيعًا فَيُنَبِّئُكُمْ بِمَا

كُنْتُمْ فِيهِ تَخْتَلِفُونَ ﴿٤٨﴾

"And we have sent down to you (O Muhammad SAW) the Book (this Qur'ân) in truth, confirming the Scripture that came before it and Muhaymin (trustworthy in highness and a witness) over it (old Scriptures). So judge among them by what Allâh has revealed, and follow not their vain desires, diverging away from the truth that has come to you. To each among you, We have prescribed a law and a clear way. <u>If Allâh had willed, He would have made you one nation, but that (He) may test you in what He has given you; so compete in good deeds. The return of</u>

you (all) is to Allâh; then He will inform you about that in which you used to differ."

So there should be no confusion in understanding that we the human beings divided into different countries, nations, creed, cultures and ethnicities, must not have cut throat competition among us. God wants us to have a healthy competition to excel in good deeds toward other peoples and nations. God commands

this because He is the
creator of all and He loves
them all.

III. HOW TO INTERPRET & UNDERSTAND THE TRUE SPIRIT OF ISLAM

Islam has circa 1.3 billion
followers worldwide. There
have been lots of
misunderstanding of Islam in
Eastern and Western
Countries. This
Misunderstanding about the
teachings of Islam and its
interaction with the people
of the book is common in all
Muslims, Christians and
Jewish. Proper understanding
of Islam is crucial and
imperative for peace and
prosperity. True and
unbiased understanding of

the teachings and spirit of
Islam will diminish the
differences, disputes,
hatred and intolerance. It
will promote amicable
attitudes and behavior,
tolerance, and a "live and
let live" way of life.
To understand the true
spirit and teachings of
Islam, we need to delve into
the Holy Quran, Hadith and
the life of the Prophet
Mohammad (saw) as an
unbiased student. Please
disregard the history of

Islam after the life of the Prophet because the history of Islam after the departure of the Prophet Mohammad (saw) from this world, may not be a true reflection of the teachings of Quran and the Prophet.

We need to study the sources of Islam; Quran, Hadith and the Life Of the Prophet Mohammad (pbuh), with reference to the context, in order to portray a true picture of Islam. When we

want to read any verse of
the Quran regarding any
specific issue, we must not
take it out of the context
and put sincere effort to
understand its meaning and
interpretation in letter and
spirit with full context.
Otherwise it may cause a
devastating misunderstanding
and delusion.

The Quran was revealed to
the Prophet in verses from
time to time and on

different occasions
considering the stages and
the circumstance in which
message of Islam was being
delivered by Him. All those
verses of the Quran were
compiled into a book, after
the life of the prophet by
his very close companions.
In short, the Prophet has
been guided and commanded by
God every inch of the way -
what, where and when to do
and what, where and when to
abstain from it. The current
order of the Quran is not

the same in which it was
revealed. However, the Quran
is still available and
preserved in its
chronological sequence form.
(See appendix 1 to see the
list of surahs of the Qur'an
in chronological order.)

We must study Quran in
chronological order vis a
vis the events of the life
of the Prophet to know the
truth about the teachings of
Islam. For example,

commandments about zakah, prohibition of drinking wine and taking interest were revealed after the establishment of the first Islamic State of Madina, during the second and third year of Hijrah.

Quran is different than usual books. It is like a dialogue. It is not only a book of instructions. It is also a narrative of how and under what circumstances the prophet of God delivered the Message of Islam to the ignorant people of his time. It also describes what Prophet and his companions endured to complete the mission. It holds all the commandments and codes of life given by God from time to time, during the dissemination of the Message that humanity should live by to be successful in this world and in the hereafter.

If we do a little research to understand the Quran in its true spirit, we will know that there are four phases of the Message. In the first phase, Prophet (pbhu) warned his friends and family that this life is temporary, God require us to worship Him alone and live with justice and peace with others. God will hold us all accountable for our deeds on the day of judgement. Whoever does good deeds will be rewarded with paradise

and those who commit sins
and bad deeds will be
punished in Hell.

In the second phase, scope
of this Message spreads to
all of the Arabian
Peninsula. The third phase
tells us that this Message
reached every corner of the
Arabia. Many tribes came to
the fold of Islam. But some
became bitter enemy of the
Messenger of God and the
Message of Islam.

The last and final phase
describes that God decided
to punish the miscreants and
arrogant non-believers. He
ordered the believers to
stand separated and
segregated from the enemies
of God. Just like He ordered
Holy Prophet Noah to build
an Ark and separate his
followers. Then God ordered
the Messenger and his
followers to inflict
punishment on the Idol
worshipers and miscreants by
waging war against them.

Just like Ferro and his gang
were defeated and perished
by the Holy Prophet Moses
and His companions. They
were punished by the swords
of the Prophet and his
followers instead of a
calamity. (See Appendix 2
for a list of significant
events in the Prophet
Mohammed's life).

IV.
Misunderstandings between the Three Religions

It is an old quotation that a little knowledge is a dangerous thing. Many people try to attribute misleading meanings to the verses of Quran to serve their own agenda intentionally or because they are just naïve. One example of the errant interpretations of the verses of Quran, due to disregard to the context and circumstances is outlined below.

Surah Maeda, verse 51 reads:

يَٰٓأَيُّهَا الَّذِينَ ءَامَنُوا لَا تَتَّخِذُوا الْيَهُودَ وَالنَّصَٰرَىٰٓ أَوْلِيَآءَ بَعْضُهُمْ أَوْلِيَآءُ بَعْضٍ وَمَن يَتَوَلَّهُم مِّنكُمْ فَإِنَّهُ مِنْهُمْ إِنَّ اللَّهَ لَا يَهْدِى الْقَوْمَ الظَّٰلِمِينَ ﴿١٥١﴾

"O, you who believe! Take not the Jews and the Christians as Auliyâ' (friends, protectors, helpers), they are but Auliyâ' of each other. And if any amongst you takes them (as Auliyâ'), then surely he is one of them. Verily, Allâh guides not those people who are the Zâlimûn (polytheists and wrong-doers and unjust)."

This surah Ma'eda was revealed in late 6 A.H. or early 7 A.H. after the treaty of Hudibeyah, when Prophet of Islam and 1400 Muslims were stopped from going to Mekkah to perform Umra. When Prophet of Islam had to sign this treaty on unfavorable terms with the non- believers and opponents of Islam. This was the final phase of the Message of God and the mission of the Prophet. All efforts by the Prophet to preach, persuade

and warn the idol worshipers
and non- believers were
exhausted. Now God decided
to punish the arrogant and
stubborn culprits. So He
ordered the Prophet and his
companions to break up with
non- believers and be
segregated and separated
from them. Just like, God
instructed Holy Prophet Noah
to build an Ark and separate
believers from non-
believers before sending
scourge and havoc in the
form of flood upon the

enemies of God. In case of
Holy Prophet Mohammad (saw),
this **punishment was
inflicted upon the**
miscreants and non-
believers by the swords of
the Prophet and his
companions. One must know
the state of affair of
Muslims and the Message of
Islam to know the truth and
understand the true Meanings
of the verses.

Both Muslims and the
People of the scripture,

based on this verse think
Muslims, Jews, and
Christians cannot be
friends. The truth is that
this verse has a time line
and it is not addressing to
the present time People of
the Book. It is meant for
only the small group of
people of that time, who
turned against the Messenger
of Allah and the Message of
Islam and were creating all
kind of hardships and
obstacles to hamper the
Message of Islam and get its

followers. It does not apply to all the generations of future.

If we staple and refer to the following verse, we might be able to understand the true spirit of the above verse. It is addressed only to a particular small group of people of that time who were arrogant and had little knowledge.

It does not apply to full spectrum of the peoples of the Book of all times. Surah

Mumtahina, verse 8 explains
this:

سُوْرَةُ الْمُمْتَحَنَة

لَا يَنْهٰكُمُ اللهُ عَنِ الَّذِيْنَ لَمْ يُقَاتِلُوْكُمْ فِى الدِّيْنِ وَلَمْ يُخْرِجُوْكُمْ

مِّنْ دِيَارِكُمْ اَنْ تَبَرُّوْهُمْ وَ تُقْسِطُوْا اِلَيْهِمْ اِنَّ اللهَ يُحِبُّ الْمُقْسِطِيْنَ

﴿٨﴾

*"Allâh does not forbid you
to deal justly and kindly
with those who fought not
against you on account of
religion nor drove you out
of your homes. Verily, Allâh
loves those who deal with
equity."*

In another place in the
Quran, it has been explained
why a group of people is

against Muslims of that
time. Surah 5 verse 82 says:

لَتَجِدَنَّ أَشَدَّ النَّاسِ عَدَاوَةً لِّلَّذِيْنَ اٰمَنُوا الْيَهُوْدَ وَالَّذِيْنَ
اَشْرَكُوْا وَلَتَجِدَنَّ اَقْرَبَهُمْ مَّوَدَّةً لِّلَّذِيْنَ اٰمَنُوا الَّذِيْنَ قَالُوْۤا
اِنَّا نَصٰرٰى ذٰلِكَ بِاَنَّ مِنْهُمْ قِسِّيْسِيْنَ وَرُهْبَانًا وَّاَنَّهُمْ لَا
يَسْتَكْبِرُوْنَ ﴿٨٢﴾

*"And you will certainly find
that the people most hostile
against the believers are
the Jews and the ones who
ascribe partners to Allah.
You will certainly find that
the closest of them in
friendship with the
believers are those who say,
'we are Christians.' That is*

85

because among them there are
priests and monks, and
because they are not
arrogant."

Here again this verse is
talking about particular
group of people of that
time. It also describes the
reason for animosity, which
is ignorance or lack of
knowledge and arrogance. It
will be quite unjust and
cruel if we generalize and
universalize it and apply it
to the people of present
time. Because over time

human beings educated
themselves, became
intellectuals and also
improved their behavior and
conduct.

The Quran also talks about
the peoples of the book of
that time, who subdued to
God and did no harm to
others. Surah 3, verse 113
reads:

لَيۡسُوۡا سَوَآءً ۚ مِّنۡ اَهۡلِ الۡكِتٰبِ اُمَّةٌ قَآىِٕمَةٌ يَّتۡلُوۡنَ اٰيٰتِ اللّٰهِ
اٰنَآءَ الَّيۡلِ وَهُمۡ يَسۡجُدُوۡنَ ﴿۱۱۳﴾

"Not all of them are alike: Among the people of the Book there are those who are steadfast; they recite the verses of Allah in the night hours, and they prostrate themselves."

The nature of interaction and relationship between the Muslims and the Peoples of the Book may be grasped by understanding the following verse, which explains that Muslims and the Peoples of the Book are not enemies or opponent or rivals of one

another. Surah 5, verse 5
reads:

اَلۡیَوۡمَ اُحِلَّ لَکُمُ الطَّیِّبٰتُ ۗ وَطَعَامُ الَّذِیۡنَ اُوۡتُوا الۡکِتٰبَ

حِلٌّ لَّکُمۡ ۪ وَطَعَامُکُمۡ حِلٌّ لَّهُمۡ ۫ وَالۡمُحۡصَنٰتُ مِنَ

الۡمُؤۡمِنٰتِ وَالۡمُحۡصَنٰتُ مِنَ الَّذِیۡنَ اُوۡتُوا الۡکِتٰبَ مِنۡ

قَبۡلِکُمۡ اِذَاۤ اٰتَیۡتُمُوۡهُنَّ اُجُوۡرَهُنَّ مُحۡصِنِیۡنَ غَیۡرَ مُسٰفِحِیۡنَ

وَلَا مُتَّخِذِیۤ اَخۡدَانٍ ؕ وَمَنۡ یَّکۡفُرۡ بِالۡاِیۡمَانِ فَقَدۡ حَبِطَ

عَمَلُهٗ ۫ وَهُوَ فِی الۡاٰخِرَةِ مِنَ الۡخٰسِرِیۡنَ ﴿۵﴾

"This day are (all) good
things made lawful for you.
The food of those who have
received the Scripture is
lawful for you, and your
food is lawful for them and

*so are the virtuous women of
the believers and the
virtuous women of those who
received the Scripture
before you (lawful for you)
when ye give them their
marriage portions and live
with them in honor, not in
fornication, nor taking them
as secret concubines.*
*Whosoever denieth the faith,
his work is vain and he will
be amongst the losers in the
Hereafter.*"

God has been commanding His
Messengers to deliver His
message to the people of
their time for a number of
years. After the conveyance

of The Message in its entirety, God asked His Prophets to separate the believers from those who did not submit to God and His Message and refuted His Messenger (prophet). Then God punished the nonbelievers. The same process was carried on during the era of Prophets Abraham, Noah, Moses and Mohammad (saw).By the same notion, in this verse, God commanded His Messenger Mohammad (saw) to segregate

believers from nonbelievers
of that time. History of
that time tells us all Jews
and Christians of that time
were not amongst the people
who ridiculed the Messenger
and the Message of God.
Matter of the fact, many
Jews and Christians embraced
the Message of God and
joined the believers. This
verse only addresses to the
small group of Jews and
Christians of that time who
were doomed and punished by
God afterwards, along with

many other nonbelievers and polytheists.

The Quran does not declare all Jews and Christians as enemy or opponent. That is why it advises the Muslims to interact and communicate with them amicably. In surah Ankaboot, verse 46, it says:

وَلَا تُجَادِلُوٓا أَهْلَ الْكِتٰبِ إِلَّا بِالَّتِى هِىَ أَحْسَنُ إِلَّا الَّذِيْنَ ظَلَمُوْا مِنْهُمْ وَقُوْلُوٓا اٰمَنَّا بِالَّذِىٓ أُنْزِلَ إِلَيْنَا وَأُنْزِلَ إِلَيْكُمْ وَإِلٰهُنَا وَإِلٰهُكُمْ وَاحِدٌ وَّنَحْنُ لَهُ مُسْلِمُوْنَ ﴿٤٦﴾

"And argue not with the people of the Scripture

*(Jews and Christians),
unless it be in (a way) that
is better (with good words
and in good manner, inviting
them to Islâmic Monotheism
with His Verses), except
with such of them as do
wrong, and say (to them):
"We believe in that which
has been revealed to us and
revealed to you; our Ilâh
(God) and your Ilâh (God) is
One (i.e. Allâh), and to Him
we have submitted (as
Muslims)."*

V. ROOTS OF

ABRAHAMIC RELIGION

We have to travel back to
history to know and
understand the stem, core
and source of the divine
religions. As we cited
above, one has to read and
interpret Quran envisaging
the historical events of the
life of the Prophet. The
Abrahamic religions are
essentially the same
religion with updates from
Holy Prophets Adam to Noah
to Abraham to Yaqoob (Jacob)
to Moses to Jesus to
Mohammad.

In surah 42, Ash-Shura verse 13, God says:

شَرَعَ لَكُمْ مِّنَ الدِّيْنِ مَا وَصّٰى بِهِ نُوْحًا وَّالَّذِيْٓ اَوْحَيْنَآ
اِلَيْكَ وَمَا وَصَّيْنَا بِهٖٓ اِبْرٰهِيْمَ وَمُوْسٰى وَعِيْسٰىٓ اَنْ اَقِيْمُوا
الدِّيْنَ وَ لَا تَتَفَرَّقُوْا فِيْهِ ۚ كَبُرَ عَلَى الْمُشْرِكِيْنَ مَا تَدْعُوْهُمْ
اِلَيْهِ ۚ اَللّٰهُ يَجْتَبِيْٓ اِلَيْهِ مَنْ يَّشَآءُ وَيَهْدِيْٓ اِلَيْهِ مَنْ يُّنِيْبُ

﴿١٣﴾

"He has ordained for you
people the same religion as
He had enjoined upon Noah,
and that which we have
revealed to you (O prophet,)
and that which we had
enjoined upon Abraham and
Moses and Jesus by saying,
"Establish the religion, and

*be not divided therein."
Arduous for the mushriks
(polytheists) is that to
which you are inviting them.
Allah chooses (and pulls)
toward Himself anyone He
wills, and guides to Himself
anyone who turns to Him (to
seek guidance)."*

Similarly, it is confirmed
that it is the same religion
in Surah 6, verse 161:

قُلْ إِنَّنِي هَدَانِي رَبِّيَ إِلَى صِرَاطٍ مُّسْتَقِيمٍ دِينًا قِيَمًا مِّلَّةَ
إِبْرَاهِيمَ حَنِيفًا وَمَا كَانَ مِنَ الْمُشْرِكِينَ ﴿١٦١﴾

*"Verily my Lord hath guided
me to a way that is*

*straight– a religion of
right– the path (trod) by
Abraham the true in Faith,
and he (certainly) joined
not gods with Allah."*

Additionally, in Surah 12,
verse 38, it is stated:

وَاتَّبَعْتُ مِلَّةَ اٰبَاۤءِیۤ اِبْرٰهِیْمَ وَاِسْحٰقَ وَیَعْقُوْبَ مَا كَانَ لَنَاۤ اَنْ

نُّشْرِكَ بِاللّٰهِ مِنْ شَیْءٍ ذٰلِكَ مِنْ فَضْلِ اللّٰهِ عَلَیْنَا وَعَلَى النَّاسِ

وَلٰكِنَّ اَكْثَرَ النَّاسِ لَا یَشْكُرُوْنَ ﴿۳۸﴾

*"And I follow the ways of my
fathers– Abraham, Isaac and
Jacob; and never
could we attribute any
partners whatever to Allah:*

that (comes) of the grace of Allah to us and to mankind: yet most men are not grateful."

Faith of the Prophet Abraham was the faith of all Prophets of God. From Adam to Noah to Abraham to Moses to Jesus to Mohammad (pbut), all believed in the same faith. The common elements of that faith are:

- Believe in Oneness of All Mighty God - There are no partners with the

God and He is all alone worthy of worship.

- Believe in all angels of God including Gabriel to Mikael to Azrael.

- Believe in all scriptures of God including Torah, Zaboor, Angeel and Quran.

- Believe in all Prophets of God from Adam to Noah to Abraham to Moses to Jesus Christ to Mohammad (pbut).

- Believe in the day of
  Judgment and that all
  deeds of virtue or vice,
  lightest to heaviest
  will be accounted for
  and rewarded or punished
  for by God in the life
  of hereafter.

VI. Completion of the Prophet's Mission

Once again visualize the kingdom of God and assimilate it with the sovereignty of the United States of America to understand it. God created all the ethnicities and races of mankind on earth. He also sent His Scriptures to be followed by the mankind as code of social conduct. So that different nations and peoples can live amicably side by side and succeed in worldly life and the life hereafter. Along

with the Scriptures, God
also sent His Messenger to
different nations from time
to time. Just like the
Ambassadors of the US
Government appointed and
sent to different countries.
These Ambassadors follow the
policies and instructions of
their home government in
letter and spirit to deal
and interact with the
peoples of those countries.
Keep in mind these
Ambassadors have only
delegated powers and are

strictly monitored by their home government. If they do not follow the guidelines of their government, they may be dismissed and grounded. *Other citizens or nationals of the home government do not have the authority of the ambassador while dealing with the people or government of other countries.*

Exactly like that, Prophets (Messengers) of God have authority and power to

disseminate the message of
God to the peoples and the
nations and sometimes
enforce the compliance of
the divine books of guidance
at the will of God. Modus
operando of the missions of
the Messengers adopted by
God was that, some prophets
were ordered by God to
preach the peoples of that
time for a number of years
and explain and demonstrate
the teachings consistently
over and over again. So that
people believe in oneness of

God, kingdom of God and the Book of guidance. Having all this done, God required compliance by the subject people. Those who subdued to God in obedience are blessed and promised reward Hereafter. But those who became stubborn, arrogant, and unruly and ridiculed the Message and the Messengers of God were punished. Some were punished right there and some will be punished in the hereafter. To fulfill his promise and to demonstrate the sovereignty of His kingdom and punish the rebels, God ordered His Messengers to wage wars against unfaithful and unruly. We know very well that Prophets do strictly what their Lord (God) wants them to do, just like Ambassadors of todays' countries. They cannot do anything on their own. They do not have any authority of their own. They have only what God gave them and their job is to perform their duty

efficiently and diligently
to please their Creator.

Here we might be able to
understand the expeditions
of the Prophets. For example
the life history of the Holy
Prophet Mohammad (saw) tells
us that He preached and
propagated the Message of
God to the people of his
time for thirteen
consecutive years. Then God
said enough is enough, time
has come to punish the
culprits and required His

Messenger to wage war
against the miscreants.

Quran's Surah Anfal verse 39
reads:

وَقَاتِلُوهُمْ حَتّٰى لَا تَكُوْنَ فِتْنَةٌ وَّيَكُوْنَ الدِّيْنُ كُلُّهُ لِلّٰهِ فَاِنِ

انْتَهَوْا فَاِنَّ اللّٰهَ بِمَا يَعْمَلُوْنَ بَصِيْرٌ ﴿٣٩﴾

*"And fight them until there
is no more Fitnah (disbelief
and polytheism: i.e.
worshipping others besides
(Allah) and the religion
(worship) will all be for
Allah Alone [in the whole of
the world]. But if they
cease (worshipping others
besides Allah), then*

certainly, Allah is All-Seer of what they do."

Again in another surah God requires the Prophet to hold the nonbelievers accountable. Surah Tawba verse 29 reads:

قَاتِلُوا الَّذِينَ لَا يُؤْمِنُوْنَ بِاللهِ وَلَا بِالْيَوْمِ الْآخِرِ وَلَا يُحَرِّمُوْنَ مَا حَرَّمَ اللهُ وَ رَسُوْلُهُ وَلَا يَدِيْنُوْنَ دِيْنَ الْحَقِّ مِنَ الَّذِيْنَ أُوْتُوا الْكِتَابَ حَتّى يُعْطُوا الْجِزْيَةَ عَنْ يَّدٍ وَّهُمْ صَغِرُوْنَ

۩٢٩۩

"Fight against those who (1) believe not in Allah, (2) nor in the Last Day, (3) nor forbid that which has been

115

forbidden by Allah and His Messenger (Muhammad saw) (4) and those who acknowledge not the religion of truth (i.e. Islam) among the people of the Scripture (Jews and Christians), until they pay the Jizyah with willing submission, and feel themselves subdued."

God uses different ways to inflict punishment on the people who deny the truth, after it has been revealed and conveyed in full to them. Sometimes He kills and wipes them off by sending calamities like earthquakes, storms, floods and droughts. For example the nation of Holy Prophet Noah. Sometimes He just gives them time until the Day of Judgment to punish them for their deeds and make them a symbol of learning the lesson. Sometimes Allah (God) uses his Prophets (Messengers) to punish the culprits, right there and then. Holy Prophet Moses kept conveying The Message to his people many years. He did his best to discharge his duties and convince his people about the truth. Some people submitted to him and became believers and companions of the Prophet. But others denied the truth and became the enemy of the Prophet Moses, his Message and his followers. God gave strength to Moses (pbuh) and established his kingdom there. After giving all the necessary means and resources to Moses (saw),

God commanded his Prophet
and his companions to punish
the culprits and finish them
all for the sake of Allah
(God). Stories and missions
of all these Prophets; Noah,
Moses, Jesus, Abraham and
many others have been quoted
and cited in the last Book
of God: Quran.

Just like Holy Prophet
Moses, last Prophet of God;
Mohammad (saw) by the order
of God, kept propagating the
Message of truth to his

people for thirteen straight
years. Many tribes of
Arabian Peninsula submitted
to God and his Message.
Peoples of these tribes
became believers and
companions of the Prophet.
God strengthened the prophet
with many powerful followers
and helped him establish his
government in the city of
Madina, Saudi Arabia.
Purpose of the rule of
Mohammad (saw) was to
establish the writ of humane
laws of peace, justice,

equality, freedom, faith in
oneness of God, his
Prophets, his Scriptures,
his angels and the day of
judgment. To uphold the
kingdom of God, Prophet
Mohammad was commanded to
wage wars one by one against
each and every   tribe in
the region until they
embrace Islam; the religion
of Prophet Abraham. Those
who did not surrender and
submit to God were punished
and marginalized. Here again
God used Prophet Mohammad

just like Prophet Moses and his followers to defeat and punish the miscreant, arrogant, unruly and the enemies of God. However, in the case of Holy Prophet Noah, God sent calamity of flood to punish the culprits of his time. Holy Prophet Jesus Christ delivered the same message of goodness. He asked his people to believe in the oneness of God, worship Him exclusively, believe in all of his prophets, his books and his angels and the day of the judgment and do good deeds. God blessed Holy Prophet Christ (pbuh) with many miracles so that He can use those miracles to deliver the Message effectively and convince his people that He is the True prophet of God and his message is the same true message of Holy Prophet Father Abraham. God knows the secret why, but He did not require Him to establish a government and punish the infidels with the help of God and his followers.

If we look at the chronological events of the life of Mohammad (saw), we see that first revelation of Quran came at the age of 40 (see appendix 2). The prophet consistently preached and disseminated the Message for 13 years until he was of the age of 53. Commandments to fight back against the stubborn and arrogant enemies of

Islam is revealed from God after 13 years of consistent preaching. The next eight years, from age 53 to 61, Prophet Mohammad and his companions were commanded to fight and punish the non-believers and oppressors. In those eight years almost twenty six expeditions were directed by God and led by the Prophet to punish and eradicate the miscreants, idol worshippers and the enemies of God who rejected and mocked the Message of truth and the source of guidance for humanity.

During these battles with different tribes of Arabia, Prophet (saw) got married to almost thirteen ladies at different times and occasions. If we research as an honest student of history, it will manifest on us that all these marriages had a reason and a purpose. Some ladies were widows, some were oppressed, some belonged to important tribes, some were influential and intelligent and some were mothers of orphans. For example one of Prophets' wife Safia (pbuh) comes of a Jewish tribe and her ancestry goes back to Holy Prophet Haroon (saw). Critics of Islam and the believers of Islam have their own reasons and arguments against and for these marriages of the Prophet.

Once again we can recall that Prophet is the messenger, servant and the ambassador of God. He does nothing on his own. His life and death is dedicated to the fulfillment of his mission. He is directed and guided all the way on each and every step by Allah (God). God commands and allows him to do certain things to succeed and accomplish his objectives. So God meant him to get married to different women to stabilize the revolution and promote confidence, peace, prosperity, and security and to defeat the bad customs & traditions of tribal culture and ignorance. Imagine how badly orphans and widows were treated in that era by the pagans. Marriages of the prophet gave protection, accommodation, status and respect to women in that society and established great relationships with the hard core tribes. Prophet

Mohammad (pbuh) married His
first wife Bibi Khadija tul
Qubra at the age of 25.
He did not marry any other
lady until the death of His
wife when after 15 years.
At the age of 40 He was
exalted to the status of
Prophet hood. Rest of His
marriages occurred during
the completion of His
mission. All of His wives
were either widows or
divorced except Bibi Aisha
Siddiqa. They all belong to
different hard core tribes.

In brief God provided all the tools, means and resources to his prophets and ambassadors to effectively carry out their assigned mission and up hold the rule of God's Kingdom.

VII. Mother of all Evils

Here comes the mother of all delusions and that is the conviction that we Muslims or Jews or Christians are chosen people and we are better than others. God says you are all equal by default. You are children of Prophet Adam (pbuh) and he was raised from mud. There is no superiority based upon ancestry or belonging to a certain Prophet or Scripture. Seniority is strictly based on the contents of each individual's actions. In worldly life criteria for seniority may be health, wealth, beauty, intelligence, influence, authority or fame. But God's criteria for seniority of human beings is exclusively based upon good deeds, piety and good contents of character.

The Quran mentions in Surah 98, verse 7

اِنَّ الَّذِيْنَ اٰمَنُوْا وَعَمِلُوا الصّٰلِحٰتِ اُولٰٓئِكَ هُمْ خَيْرُ الْبَرِيَّةِ ۚ

﴿٧﴾

"Verily, those who believe and do righteous good deeds, they are the best of creatures."

Again in Surah 49, Verse 13 God declares

يَٰٓأَيُّهَا ٱلنَّاسُ إِنَّا خَلَقْنَٰكُم مِّن ذَكَرٍ وَّأُنثَىٰ وَجَعَلْنَٰكُمْ شُعُوبًا

وَّقَبَآئِلَ لِتَعَارَفُوٓا۟ إِنَّ أَكْرَمَكُمْ عِندَ ٱللَّهِ أَتْقَىٰكُمْ إِنَّ ٱللَّهَ

عَلِيمٌ خَبِيرٌ ﴿١٣﴾

"O mankind, We have created you from a male and a female, and made you into races and tribes, so that you may identify one another. Surely the noblest of you, in Allah's sight, is the one who is most pious of you. Surely Allah is All-Knowing, All-Aware."

Some of us who are ignorant and arrogant they think that

they Have special relationship with God. They are better than others and they have been granted the license / permit to launch expeditions against those who are wrong-doers and do not believe in what they do and do not follow the religion they do. This is a very dangerous and a devastating ideology. The truth is that we are not the prophets. We are the creation and servants of

God. Our job is not to enforce the compliance of the religion of Abraham. Only the Prophets were assigned this job.

For us, Quran says in surah 29, verse 46:

وَلَا تُجَادِلُوٓا اَهْلَ الْكِتٰبِ اِلَّا بِالَّتِي هِيَ اَحْسَنُ اِلَّا الَّذِيْنَ ظَلَمُوْا مِنْهُمْ وَقُوْلُوٓا اٰمَنَّا بِالَّذِيٓ اُنْزِلَ اِلَيْنَا وَاُنْزِلَ اِلَيْكُمْ وَاِلٰهُنَا وَاِلٰهُكُمْ وَاحِدٌ وَّنَحْنُ لَهٗ مُسْلِمُوْنَ ﴿٤٦﴾

"And argue not with the people of the Scripture

(Jews and Christians in good manner, inviting them to Islamic Monotheism with His Verses), except with such of them as do wrong, and say (to them): "We believe in that which has been revealed to us and revealed to you; our Allah (God) and your God is One, and to Him we have submitted (as Muslims)."

At another place Quran says in surah 2 verse 256

لَآ إِكْرَاهَ فِى الدِّيْنِ ۖ قَد تَّبَيَّنَ الرُّشْدُ مِنَ الْغَيِّ ۚ فَمَن يَّكْفُرْ بِالطَّاغُوتِ وَيُؤْمِنْ بِاللّٰهِ فَقَدِ اسْتَمْسَكَ بِالْعُرْوَةِ الْوُثْقٰى ۖ لَا انْفِصَامَ لَهَا ۚ وَاللّٰهُ سَمِيْعٌ عَلِيْمٌ ﴿٢٥٧﴾

"Let there be no compulsion in religion. Truth stands out clear from Error; whoever rejects Evil and believes in Allah hath grasped the most trustworthy hand-hold, that never breaks. And Allah hears and knows all things."

What is our job then, being the servant of God and well-wisher of all the people. We

142

can invite our fellow human beings to the last message of God, in the best possibly polite, sincere and compassionate way. The Quran in surah 3 verse 104 refers to this activity as

وَلْتَكُن مِّنكُمْ أُمَّةٌ يَّدْعُونَ إِلَى الْخَيْرِ وَيَأْمُرُونَ بِالْمَعْرُوفِ وَيَنْهَوْنَ عَنِ الْمُنكَرِ ۚ وَأُولَٰئِكَ هُمُ الْمُفْلِحُونَ ﴿١٠٤﴾

"Let there arise out of you a band of people inviting to all that is good, enjoining what is right, and forbidding what is wrong;

they are the ones to attain felicity."

Some people misunderstand the scope of this verse and derive the meanings of armed struggle against wrong doers from it. If the individuals and small groups start doing this by force, they will do much more bad than good. It is like penny wise pound foolish. First of all they do not have any mandate or legal and legitimate authority to enforce the

goodness and righteousness.
Secondly, who are we to pass
judgment and give decree to
punish the wrong doers. This
authority rests with the
God.

Even the Prophets of God had
no authority to punish the
disbelievers until commanded
by God. Their primary
function was to invite,
preach and demonstrate the
word and message of God.

For example Prophet Jesus Christ only preached and conveyed the message of God to his peoples. He was not required by the All Mighty to punish those who did not submit to the God and his messenger.

Surah 34, verse 28 cites the primary role of Prophets

وَمَآ أَرْسَلْنَٰكَ إِلَّا كَآفَّةً لِّلنَّاسِ بَشِيرًا وَنَذِيرًا وَّلَٰكِنَّ أَكْثَرَ النَّاسِ لَا يَعْلَمُونَ ﴿٢٨﴾

"We have not sent thee but as a (Messenger) to men, giving them Glad tidings, and warning them (against sin), but most men understand not."

In the cases of Prophet Mohammad (saw) and Prophet Moses (saw) this decision to punish the wrong doers was made by God at a suitable time after exhausting the Prophets efforts to invite people to the fold of God's blessings. If any group tries to do the job of prophets and launch any offensive or expedition against others who they think are not on the right path, they will be miscreants and cause mischief, chaos, unrest and upheaval in society.

Forbidding evil means stopping and hindering the evil which falls within the purview of your discretion, influence, jurisdiction and authority. For example parents have their influence

and authority over their
kids and they can stop and
forbid them from wrong
doings. Same way teachers
have authority and influence
over their students in
school to keep them from
bad things and deeds. In the
work place, the boss has
some control over his
employees and subordinates
to admonish and prevent them
from bad practices and
actions. Beyond that local,
state and federal
governments have authority

over their citizens to
enforce compliance of the
laws of the land. They can
make their citizens to stop
at red light and drive at
green light. They can use
force to hold and punish
the law breakers. Government
has jurisdiction and
authority to forbid their
citizens from wrong doings.
When peoples or groups of
people act beyond the
jurisdiction of their
authority to enjoin good and
forbid evil, this is where

they make fatal blunder and
cause mischief (fitna).They
think they are striving for
the good but matter of the
fact they are paving the way
of evil and anarchy.

The Quran addresses actions
of those people who are
actually fool friends and
hence are worse than foes.
They are not friends of God.
They are rather enemies of
God. They create mischief
instead of peace and

harmony. In surah 26 verse
183, God says

وَلَا تَبْخَسُوا النَّاسَ أَشْيَاءَهُمْ وَلَا تَعْثَوْا فِي الْأَرْضِ مُفْسِدِينَ

﴿١٨٣﴾

*"And withhold not things
justly due to men, nor do
evil in the land, working
mischief."*

Again Allah enjoins at
another place in Quran
In surah 28, verse 77 God
commands

وَابْتَغِ فِيمَآ أَتَلكَ اللّهُ الدَّارَ الْأَخِرَةَ وَلَا تَنسَ نَصِيبَكَ مِنَ

الدُّنْيَا وَأَحْسِن كَمَآ أَحْسَنَ اللّهُ إِلَيْكَ وَلَا تَبْغِ الْفَسَادَ فِي

الْأَرْضِ إِنَّ اللّهَ لَا يُحِبُّ الْمُفْسِدِينَ ﴿٧٧﴾

"But seek, with the (wealth) which Allah has bestowed on thee, the Home of the Hereafter, nor forget thy portion in this world: but do thou good, as Allah has been good to thee, and seek not (occasions for) mischief in the land: for Allah loves not those who do mischief." These independent militant groups who act on their own and have no respect

for their governments, are
challenging the writ of the
Government and ridiculing
the laws of the land. They
may be sincere and faithful
to their respective
religion. But they are
stubborn, and ignorant. They
are being misguided by their
few clerks because of their
lack of knowledge and
ignorance. They do not know
that these clerks are
twisting their religion in
hatred and frustration.

These militant clerks flex
muscles to manipulate and
black mail legitimate
governments of the peoples
at large and become power
brokers. None of the divine
religions; Judaism,
Christianity or Islam
endorses and encourages such
behavior and struggle. They
are arrant fools. They think
they are serving their
religion and their God. But
in reality they are
committing heinous crimes
and sins. Sanctity of human

life is unquestionable and
uncompromisable.

In surah 5, verse 32 of the
Quran

مِنْ اَجْلِ ذٰلِكَ ۛ كَتَبْنَا عَلٰى بَنِيٓ اِسْرَآءِيْلَ

اَنَّهٗ مَنْ قَتَلَ نَفْسًۢا بِغَيْرِ نَفْسٍ اَوْ فَسَادٍ فِى الْاَرْضِ فَكَاَنَّمَا

قَتَلَ النَّاسَ جَمِيْعًا ۗ وَمَنْ اَحْيَاهَا فَكَاَنَّمَآ اَحْيَا النَّاسَ

جَمِيْعًا ۗ وَلَقَدْ جَآءَتْهُمْ رُسُلُنَا بِالْبَيِّنٰتِ ثُمَّ اِنَّ كَثِيْرًا مِّنْهُمْ

بَعْدَ ذٰلِكَ فِى الْاَرْضِ لَمُسْرِفُوْنَ ﴿٣٢﴾

*"On that account: We
ordained for the Children of
Israel that if anyone slew a
person-unless it be for*

156

*murder or for spreading
mischief in the land– it
would be as if he slew the
whole people: and if anyone
saved a life it would be as
if he saved the life of the
whole people. Then although
there came to them Our
Messengers with clear Signs,
yet even after that many of
them continued to commit
excesses in the land."*

In Surah 28 Verse 83, God
warns the rebels of the
consequences in the
hereafter for spreading
mischief in the land.

تِلْكَ الدَّارُ الْأَخِرَةُ نَجْعَلُهَا لِلَّذِينَ لَا يُرِيدُونَ عُلُوًّا فِي الْأَرْضِ وَلَا فَسَادًا ۚ وَالْعَاقِبَةُ لِلْمُتَّقِينَ ﴿٨٣﴾

"That home of the Hereafter (i.e. Paradise), we shall assign to those who rebel not against the truth with pride and oppression in the land nor do mischief by committing crimes. And the good end is for the Muttaqûn (pious righteous persons - see V.2:2)."

We can use our moral authority to persuade and goad other peoples to

158

goodness and forbid from evil. This can be done by initiating and engaging logical, sincere and compassionate dialogue and discussion or by setting examples of high moral character. It can also be done by influencing and inspiring by recognizing and rewarding high moral values and good deeds.

Education, awareness and training of character can play a major role in

achieving this goal. Also
people can only disseminate
and propagate the
Message of God and of His
Prophets, to promote good
deed and abstain from wrong
doings. Fellow citizens
cannot put others on the
path of guidance and
righteousness. Only God can
enlighten their hearts.

In surah 28 ayah 56, God
tells us that nobody can
give guidance and put on the
right path except Him:

إِنَّكَ لَا تَهْدِى مَنْ أَحْبَبْتَ وَلَكِنَّ اللهَ يَهْدِى مَنْ يَّشَآءُ وَهُوَ

أَعْلَمُ بِالْمُهْتَدِينَ ﴿٥٧﴾

"You cannot give guidance to whomsoever you wish, but Allah gives guidance to whomsoever He wills, and He best knows the ones who are on the right path."

Again at another place in Quran, surah 39 verse 41, God says

إِنَّا أَنْزَلْنَا عَلَيْكَ الْكِتَابَ لِلنَّاسِ بِالْحَقِّ فَمَنِ اهْتَدَى فَلِنَفْسِهِ وَمَنْ ضَلَّ فَإِنَّمَا يَضِلُّ عَلَيْهَا وَمَا أَنْتَ عَلَيْهِمْ بِوَكِيلٍ

﴿٤١﴾

"We have sent down to you the Book for the people with truth. So, whoever follows the guidance, it is for his own good, and whoever goes astray, he will go astray only to his own detriment – and you are not responsible for them."

The use of force is not permissible and it cannot produce any positive results. Compulsion and

force can defeat the purpose
and may cause hate and
animosity.

In surah 2 verse 256 God
says:

لَآ إِكْرَاهَ فِى الدِّيْنِ ۛ قَد تَّبَيَّنَ الرُّشْدُ مِنَ الْغَيِّ ۚ فَمَنْ يَّكْفُرْ

بِالطَّاغُوْتِ وَيُؤْمِنْ بِاللّٰهِ فَقَدِ اسْتَمْسَكَ بِالْعُرْوَةِ الْوُثْقٰى ۗ لَا

انْفِصَامَ لَهَا ۗ وَاللّٰهُ سَمِيْعٌ عَلِيْمٌ ﴿٢٥٦﴾

"Let there be no compulsion
in religion. Truth stands
out clear from Error;
whoever rejects Evil and
believes in Allah hath
grasped the most trustworthy

*hand-hold, which never
breaks. And Allah heareth
and knoweth all things."*

Use of force to forbid the
evil is permissible only if
this evil is damaging the
lives, property and honor of
public at large. Now the
question arises, who can use
that force? Answer is the
Government of the people.
Only Government has the
legitimate authority to use
the proportionate force to
curb the evil. If
individuals and groups do

this job, they will do more
harm than good and cause
chaos, disobedience and
lawlessness in the society.

VIII.Writ of the Government

Only the Government of a
people has the legitimate
authority_and mandate to use
force against law breakers
and wrong doers. That is why

we have police and criminal justice systems in place in our countries. If individuals and groups could do this on their own without creating mischief and chaos, we would not need police in our societies and countries. As a matter of fact, we give up lot of our freedoms and pleasures to collective discipline in exchange for peace and for protection of human rights.

we obey and abide by the laws of the land and subdue to the rule and authority of the Government, so that we can enjoy peace, reasonable freedom, safety and prosperity. Individuals and groups have only moral authority to invite, motivate and persuade others to do good deeds and abstain from evil practices.

After obeying God and his Messenger, it is imperative and obligatory upon the

citizens to obey their
rulers and Government.
God commands human beings

In Surah 4 Verse 59

يَـٰٓأَيُّهَا الَّذِينَ ءَامَنُوٓا أَطِيعُوا اللّٰهَ وَأَطِيعُوا الرَّسُولَ وَأُولِى
الْأَمْرِ مِنكُمْ ۖ فَإِن تَنَازَعْتُمْ فِى شَىْءٍ فَرُدُّوهُ إِلَى اللّٰهِ وَالرَّسُولِ
إِن كُنتُمْ تُؤْمِنُونَ بِاللّٰهِ وَالْيَوْمِ الْآخِرِ ۚ ذَٰلِكَ خَيْرٌ وَّأَحْسَنُ
تَأْوِيلًا ﴿٥٩﴾

*"O ye who believe! Obey
Allah, and obey the
messenger and those of you
who are in authority; and if
ye have a dispute concerning
any matter, refer it to
Allah and the messenger if*

*ye are (in truth) believers
in Allah and the Last Day.
That is better and more
seemly in the end."*

God created and crafted this
world and its creature
including mankind in the
best possible way. He does
not want anyone to disturb
and damage this world and
its inhabitants. So He
ordered Man-kind to respect
and follow their leaders and
rulers. Because this is
perhaps the only way to
keeping this world moving

forward progressively, smoothly and peacefully. It is a major sin to cause disorder in society and country. Some peoples or groups turn against the government pleading that their Government is corrupt. This is understandable that these peoples are disappointed and frustrated by the performance of these Governments over many decades. God will not accept any such excuses to use force against the government. Because such a violent struggle against the rulers will do much more harm than good to the common man and public at large. It will create a general disorder, chaos and disruption in the society and jeopardize the safety and sanctity of life, honor and property of citizens of the country without producing any positive results.

In this era of civilized world, we have independent electronic and print media like the internet, television, radio and newspapers. We have national and international justice system, civil society and above all most of our Governments are democratic. The best bet to get rid of the corrupt Governments is to take part in the democratic process and build public opinion and support in favor of sincere, honest and knowledgeable candidates and hence bring about a positive change in the Government. We can over through corrupt Governments with the power of the vote by mobilizing social media and building public opinion. For example, in parliamentary democracy, a corrupt, unjust and cruel Prime Minister or Head of the State can be removed by passing vote of no confidence motion in the House. In presidential democracy, such a bad president can be removed by impeachment.

People who invest all their human and financial resources to struggle peacefully without resorting to violence will win the heart of the public and approval of God, the most merciful the most magnificent. Then God will help them to succeed in their noble mission and bring about a positive

change by over throwing the
corrupt   Government
peacefully   and
democratically. God actually
commands us to resolve our
disputes democratically.

In surah 42 verse 38 God
warns us that those who run
their affairs and settle
their   disputes
democratically   with
consultation   will   also
succeed in the hereafter.

وَالَّذِينَ اسْتَجَابُوا لِرَبِّهِمْ وَأَقَامُوا الصَّلٰوةَ ۚ وَأَمْرُهُمْ شُوْرٰى

بَيْنَهُمْ ۚ وَمِمَّا رَزَقْنٰهُمْ يُنْفِقُوْنَ ﴿٣٨﴾

"Those who harken to their Lord, and establish regular prayer; who (conduct) their affairs by mutual Consultation; who spend out of what We bestow on them for Sustenance."

In short, armed struggles against a Government, especially a democratic government, is strictly forbidden and haram.

Now there is another angle to the armed struggle. Those who engage in armed struggle do not have any regard for the lives of innocent peoples and their property. It is very deplorable that they call it *'collateral damage'* and have no remorse or regret for that. They are just ignorant, misguided, callous and arrogant. They have little knowledge and no fear of God and the Day of Judgment when all actions of peoples will be weighed and accounted for.

In Quran's surah 99 verse 7&8

فَمَن يَّعْمَلْ مِثْقَالَ ذَرَّةٍ خَيْرًا يَّرَهُ ۝ وَمَن يَّعْمَلْ مِثْقَالَ ذَرَّةٍ شَرًّا يَّرَهُ ۝

"So whosoever does good equal to the weight of an atom (or a small ant), shall see it (7). And whosoever does evil equal to the weight of an atom (or a small ant), shall see it (8)."

God heralds that in the here-after, He will reckon all the deeds even the tiniest, of people for reward of Paradise or punishment of Hell. But these naïve rebels perish lives and property of innocent people in the name of collateral damage.

If we revisit the life history of the last Prophet of God, we learn that in all the expeditions he led during his life time, He required His companions not to kill anyone who is a noncombatant. Even a combatant cannot be killed if he surrenders in the battle field. He can be arrested though. Women, children, sick and elderly are not to be forced in war. Property of masses cannot be damaged. Trees, animals and water resources cannot be destroyed.

The same principals and rules were adopted 14

centuries later, after world war second, in the fourth treaty of Geneva Convention of 1949. It was signed by 195 nations of the world, agreeing to abide by these moral values

in war and peace and that they will be accountable and can be disciplined and punishment by international community for any violation.

In surah Nisa Verse 93, God says

وَمَن يَقْتُلْ مُؤْمِنًا مُّتَعَمِّدًا فَجَزَآؤُهُ جَهَنَّمُ خَالِدًا فِيهَا وَغَضِبَ اللَّهُ عَلَيْهِ وَلَعَنَهُ وَأَعَدَّ لَهُ عَذَابًا عَظِيمًا ﴿٩٣﴾

"whoever kills a believer deliberately, his reward is Jahannam (Hell) where he shall remain forever, and Allah shall be angry with him and shall cast curse upon him, and He has prepared for him a mighty punishment."

In surah 28 ayah 83, God clarifies this

تِلْكَ الدَّارُ الْآخِرَةُ نَجْعَلُهَا لِلَّذِينَ لَا يُرِيدُونَ عُلُوًّا فِي الْأَرْضِ وَلَا فَسَادًا ۚ وَالْعَاقِبَةُ لِلْمُتَّقِينَ ﴿٨٣﴾

"As for that Ultimate Abode (the Hereafter), We assign it to those who do not intend haughtiness on earth nor mischief. And the (best) end is for the God-fearing."

In the same surah ayah 77, once again Allah says

185

وَابْتَغِ فِيمَا آتَاكَ اللّٰهُ الدَّارَ الْآخِرَةَ وَلَا تَنْسَ نَصِيبَكَ مِنَ الدُّنْيَا وَأَحْسِنْ كَمَا أَحْسَنَ اللّٰهُ إِلَيْكَ وَلَا تَبْغِ الْفَسَادَ فِي الْأَرْضِ إِنَّ اللّٰهَ لَا يُحِبُّ الْمُفْسِدِينَ ﴿٧٧﴾

"But seek, with that (wealth) which Allâh has bestowed on you, the home of the Hereafter, and forget not your portion of lawful enjoyment in this world, and do good as Allâh has been good to you, and seek not mischief in the land. Verily, Allâh likes not the Mufsidûn (those who commit great crimes and sins, oppressors, tyrants,

mischief-makers,
corrupters)."

REFERENCES

1. Publications of Al Mawrid Institute

2. Website Easy Islam

3. Website Quran Explorer

4. Website Tanzeel

5. Islamic code of life by professor Khurshid Ahmed

6. Lectures of great research scholar Javed Ahmed Ghamdi

7. Lectures of Dr. Israr Ahmed

8. Geo tv debates

9. ARY tv debates

10. Maryland Public Television

11. CNN

12. Last Divine Book of Guidance- AL Quran

APPENDIX 1

The chronological order in which the Holy Quran was revealed:

Chronological Order	Surah Name	Number of Verses	Location of Revelation	Traditional Order
1	Al-Alaq	19	Mecca	96
2	Al-Qalam	52	Mecca	68
3	Al-Muzzammil	20	Mecca	73

Chronological Order	Surah Name	Number of Verses	Location of Revelation	Traditional Order
4	Al-Muddathir	56	Mecca	74
5	Al-Fatiha	7	Mecca	1
6	Al-Masadd	5	Mecca	111
7	At-Takwir	29	Mecca	81
8	Al-Ala	19	Mecca	87

Chronological Order	Surah Name	Number of Verses	Location of Revelation	Traditional Order
9	Al-Lail	21	Mecca	92
10	Al-Fajr	30	Mecca	89
11	Ad-Dhuha	11	Mecca	93
12	Al-Inshirah	8	Mecca	94
13	Al-Asr	3	Mecca	103
14	Al-Adiyat	11	Mecca	100

Chronological Order	Surah Name	Number of Verses	Location of Revelation	Traditional Order
15	Al-Kauther	3	Mecca	108
16	At-Takathur	8	Mecca	102
17	Al-Maun	7	Mecca	107
18	Al-Kafiroon	6	Mecca	109
19	Al-Fil	5	Mecca	105
20	Al-Falaq	5	Mecca	113

Chronological Order	Surah Name	Number of Verses	Location of Revelation	Traditional Order
21	An-Nas	6	Mecca	114
22	Al-Ikhlas	4	Mecca	112
23	An-Najm	62	Mecca	53
24	Abasa	42	Mecca	80
25	Al-Qadr	5	Mecca	97
26	Ash-Shams	15	Mecca	91

Chronological Order	Surah Name	Number of Verses	Location of Revelation	Traditional Order
27	Al-Burooj	22	Mecca	85
28	At-Tin	8	Mecca	95
29	Quraish	4	Mecca	106
30	Al-Qaria	11	Mecca	101
31	Al-Qiyama	40	Mecca	75
32	Al-Humaza	9	Mecca	104

Chronological Order	Surah Name	Number of Verses	Location of Revelation	Traditional Order
33	Al-Mursalat	50	Mecca	77
34	Qaf	45	Mecca	50
35	Al-Balad	20	Mecca	90
36	At-Tariq	17	Mecca	86
37	Al-Qamar	55	Mecca	54
38	Sad	88	Mecca	38

Chronological Order	Surah Name	Number of Verses	Location of Revelation	Traditional Order
39	Al-Araf	206	Mecca	7
40	Al-Jinn	28	Mecca	72
41	Ya-Sin	83	Mecca	36
42	Al-Furqan	77	Mecca	25
43	Fatir	45	Mecca	35
44	Maryam	98	Mecca	19
45	Taha	135	Mecca	20

Chronological Order	Surah Name	Number of Verses	Location of Revelation	Traditional Order
46	Al-Waqia	96	Mecca	56
47	Ash-Shuara	226	Mecca	26
48	An-Naml	93	Mecca	27
49	Al-Qasas	88	Mecca	28
50	Al-Isra	111	Mecca	17
51	Yunus	109	Mecca	10

Chrono logical Order	Surah Name	Number of Verses	Location of Revelation	Traditional Order
52	Hud	123	Mecca	11
53	Yusuf	111	Mecca	12
54	Al-Hijr	99	Mecca	15
55	Al-Anaam	165	Mecca	6
56	As-Saaffat	182	Mecca	37
57	Luqman	34	Mecca	31

Chronological Order	Surah Name	Number of Verses	Location of Revelation	Traditional Order
58	Saba	54	Mecca	34
59	Az-Zumar	75	Mecca	39
60	Al-Ghafir	85	Mecca	40
61	Fussilat	54	Mecca	41
62	Ash-Shura	53	Mecca	42
63	Az-Zukhruf	89	Mecca	43

Chronological Order	Surah Name	Number of Verses	Location of Revelation	Traditional Order
64	Ad-Dukhan	59	Mecca	44
65	Al-Jathiya	37	Mecca	45
66	Al-Ahqaf	35	Mecca	46
67	Adh-Dhariyat	60	Mecca	51
68	Al-Ghashiya	26	Mecca	88
69	Al-Kahf	110	Mecca	18

Chrono logical Order	Surah Name	Number of Verses	Location of Revelation	Traditional Order
70	An-Nahl	128	Mecca	16
71	Nooh	28	Mecca	71
72	Ibrahim	52	Mecca	14
73	Al-Ambiya	112	Mecca	21
74	Al-Mumenoon	118	Mecca	23
75	As-Sajda	30	Mecca	32

Chronological Order	Surah Name	Number of Verses	Location of Revelation	Traditional Order
76	At-Tur	49	Mecca	52
77	Al-Mulk	30	Mecca	67
78	Al-Haaqqa	52	Mecca	69
79	Al-Maarij	44	Mecca	70
80	An-Naba	40	Mecca	78
81	An-Naziat	46	Mecca	79

Chronological Order	Surah Name	Number of Verses	Location of Revelation	Traditional Order
82	Al-Infitar	19	Mecca	82
83	Al-Inshiqaq	25	Mecca	84
84	Ar-Room	60	Mecca	30
85	Al-Ankaboot	69	Mecca	29
86	Al-Mutaffifin	36	Mecca	83
87	Al-Baqara	286	Medina	2

Chronological Order	Surah Name	Number of Verses	Location of Revelation	Traditional Order
88	Al-Anfal	75	Medina	8
89	Al-i-Imran	200	Medina	3
90	Al-Ahzab	73	Medina	33
91	Al-Mumtahina	13	Medina	60
92	An-Nisa	176	Medina	4
93	Al-	8	Medina	99

Chronological Order	Surah Name	Number of Verses	Location of Revelation	Traditional Order
	Zalzala			
94	Al-Hadid	29	Medina	57
95	Muhammad	38	Medina	47
96	Ar-Rad	43	Medina	13
97	Al-Rahman	78	Medina	55
98	Al-Insan	31	Medina	76

Chronological Order	Surah Name	Number of Verses	Location of Revelation	Traditional Order
99	At-Talaq	12	Medina	65
100	Al-Bayyina	8	Medina	98
101	Al-Hashr	24	Medina	59
102	An-Noor	64	Medina	24
103	Al-Hajj	78	Medina	22
104	Al-Munafiqoon	11	Medina	63

Chronological Order	Surah Name	Number of Verses	Location of Revelation	Traditional Order
105	Al-Mujadila	22	Medina	58
106	Al-Hujraat	18	Medina	49
107	At-Tahrim	12	Medina	66
108	At-Taghabun	18	Medina	64
109	As-Saff	14	Medina	61

Chronological Order	Surah Name	Number of Verses	Location of Revelation	Traditional Order
110	Al-Jumua	11	Medina	62
111	Al-Fath	29	Medina	48
112	Al-Maeda	120	Medina	5
113	At-Taubah	129	Medina	9
114	An-Nasr	3	Medina	110

APPENDIX 2

Chronology of Events in the Life of Muhammad (P.B.U.H)

Brief Description of the Event	Approximate Date Age of the Holy Prophet according to Lunar Calendar	Approximate Gregorian and Hijra dates BH=Before Hijra, AH=After Hijra
The Holy Prophet of Islam, Muhammad, peace be upon him, born an orphan His father Abdullah, may Allah be pleased with him, had died a few months before the	0 years	9 or 12 Rabi-ul-Awwal 52 or 53 BH April 570 or 571 AD

birth of his son.		
Hadrat Halima Sadiyya, may Allah be pleased with her, appointed wet nurse.	8 days	
Return to Mecca under the care of his mother	6 Years	46 BH 577 AD
Mother, Hadrat Amina, may Allah be pleased with her, passes away	6 Years	46 BH 577 AD
Grandfather, Hadrat Abdul-Muttalib, may Allah be	8 Years	44 BH 579 AD

pleased with him, died		
First visit to Syria with a trading caravan 12 years 40 BH, 583 AD	12 Years	40 BH 583 AD
Pledge of Fudul to help the needy and the oppressed	15 Years	37 BH 586 AD
Second journey to Syria for trade as an agent of Hadrat Khadija, may Allah be pleased with her	25 Years	28 BH 595 AD

Marriage with Hadrat Khadija, may Allah be pleased with her	25 Years	28 BH 595 AD
Birth of a son, Hadrat Qasim (may Allah be pleased with him)	28 Years	25 BH 598 AD
Birth of his daughter, Hadrat Zainab, may Allah be pleased with her	30 Years	23 BH 600 AD
Birth of his daughter, Hadrat Ruqayya, may Allah be	33 Years	20 BH 603 AD

pleased with her		
Birth of his daughter, Hadrat Um-e-Kalthum, may Allah be pleased with her	34 years	19 BH 604 AD
Renovation of Ka'aba and the placement of Hajr-e-Aswad (Black Stone)	35 years	18 BH 605 AD
Birth of his daughter, Hadrat Fatima, may Allah be pleased with her	35 years	18 BH605 AD
Hadrat Jibrail bought the	40 Year	12 BH 610

		AD
First Revelation in the Cave of Hira		
Revelation of the Holy Quran continues, Ministry of the Holy Prophet Muhammad (peace be upon him) is established. Hadrat Khadija (the wife), Hadrat Abu Bakr (the best friend), Hadrat Ali (the dearest cousin) and Hadrat Zaid (a freed slave and adopted son), may	40 Years 6 months	Friday 18 Ramadan 12 BH 14 August 610 AD

Allah be pleased with them all, accept Islam		
Open invitation to the people of Mecca to join Islam under Allah's command	43 Years	9 BH 614 AD
A group of Muslims emigrates to Abyssinia	46 Years	7 BH 615 AD
Blockade of Shi'b Abi-Talib	46 Years	7 BH 30 September 615 AD
Hadrat Hamza (paternal uncle) and Hadrat Umar,	46 Years	6 BH 616 AD

may Allah be pleased with them, accept Islam		
Hadrat Abu Talib, (beloved uncle and guardian) and only a few days later, Hadrat Khadija, the most beloved wife, may Allah be pleased with them, passed away	49 Years	Ramadan 3 BH January 619 AD
Marriage with Hadrat Sau'da, (May Allah be pleased with her)	49 Years	3 BH 619 AD

Marriage with Hadrat Aisha, may Allah be pleased with her	49 Years	3 BH 619 AD
Journey to Ta'if, about 40 miles from Mecca, for calling the citizens of Ta'if to Islam	49 Years	3 BH 619 AD
Journey of Mi'raj. Five daily prayers made obligatory for Muslims	50 Years	27 Rajab 2 BH 8 March 620 AD
Deputation from Medina accepts Islam	50 Years	2 BH 620 AD

First Pledge of 'Aq'ba'	52 Years	Dhul Haj, 1 BH 621 AD
Second Pledge of 'Aq'ba	52 Years	3 months BH June 622 AD
Hijra (migration) from Mecca to the cave of Thaur	52 Years	Friday 27 Safar 10 September 622
Emigration to Medina begins	52 Years	Monday 1 Rabi-ul-Awwal 13 September 622 AD
Arrival at Medina after the first Friday Prayer at Quba's Mosque	53 Years	12 Rabi-ul-Awwal 1st year AH 24 September 622 AD

Construction of the Holy Prophet's Mosque at Medina. Hadrat Bilal's call for Prayer (Adhan)	53 Years	1st year AH 622 AD
Brotherhood pacts between Ansar (Muslims from Medina) and Muhajirin (immigrants from Mecca)	53 Years	1st year AH 622 AD
Treaty with Jews of Medina	53 Years	1st year AH 622 AD
Permission to fight in self-defense is granted by Allah	53 Years	12 Safar 2 AH 14 August 623 AD

Ghazwa (Battle) of Waddan	53 Years	29 Safar 2 AH 31 August 623
Ghazwa (Battle) of Safwan	54 Years	2 AH 623 AD
Ghazwa (Battle) Dul-'Ashir	54 Years	2 AH 623 AD
Hadrat Salman Farsi, may Allah be pleased with him, accepts Islam	54 Years	2 AH 624 AD
Revelation and change of Qibla (direction to face for Formal	54 Years	Sha'abn 2 AH February 624 AD

Prayers, Salat) towards Ka'ba Fasting in the month of Ramadan becomes obligatory		
Ghazwa (Battle) of Badr	54 Years	12-17 Ramadan 2 AH March 8-13, 624 AD
Ghazwa (Battle) of Bani Salim	54 Years	25 Ramadan 2 AH 21 March 524 AD
Initiation of Eid-ul-Fitr and Zakat-ul-Fitr (Alms at the Eid-ul-Fitr).	54 Years	28 Ramadan / 1 Shawwal 2 AH 24/25 March 624 AD

Zakat becomes obligatory for Muslims	54 Years	Shawwal 2 AH April 624 AD
Nikah and Marriage ceremony of Hadrat Fatima, may Allah be pleased with her	54 Years	Shawwal 2 AH April 624 AD
Ghazwa (Battle) of Bani Qainuqa	54 Years	15 Shawwal 2 AH 10 April 624 AD
Ghazwa (Battle) of Sawiq	54 Years	5 Dhul-Haj 2 AH 29 May 624 AD
Ghazwa (Battle) of Ghatfan	54 Years	Muharram 3 AH July 624 AD

Ghazwa (Battle) of Bahran	55 Years	Rabi-us-Sani 3 AH October 624 AD
Marriage with Hadrat Hafsa, may Allah be pleased with her	55 Years	Shaban 3 AH January 625 AD
Ghazwa (Battle) of Uhad	55 Years	6 Shawwal 3 AH 22 March 625
Ghazwa (Battle) of Humra-ul-Asad	55 Years	8 Shawwal 3 AH 24 March 625 AD
Marriage with Hadrat Zainab Bint Khazima, may Allah be pleased with her	55 Years	Dhul-Haj 3 AH May 625 AD

Ghazwa (Battle) of Banu Nudair	56 Years	Rabi-ul-Awwal 4 AH August 625 AD
Prohibition of Drinking in Islam	56 Years	Rabi-ul-Awwal 4 AH August 625 AD
Ghazwa (Battle) of Dhatur-Riqa	56 Years	Jamadi-ul-Awwal 4 AH October 625 AD
Marriage with Hadrat Um-e-Salma, may Allah be pleased with her	56 Years	Shawwal 4 AH March 626 AD
Ghazwa (Battle) of Badru-Ukhra	56 Years	Dhul Qad 4 AH April 626

Ghazwa (Battle) of Dumatul-Jandal	57 Years	25 Rabi-ul-Awwal 5 AH
Ghazwa (Battle) of Banu Mustalaq Nikah with Hadrat Jawariya bint Harith, may Allah be pleased with her	57 Years	3 Shaban 5 AH 28 December 626 AD
Marriage with Hadrat Zainab bint Hajash, may Allah be pleased with her	57 Years	Shawwal 5 AH February 627 AD
Revelation for Hijab, rules of modesty	57 Years	1 Dhi Qa'd 5 AH 24 March 627

		AD
Ghazwa (Battle) of Ahzab or Khandaq (Ditch)	57 Years	8 Dhi Qa'd 5 AH 31 March 627 AD
Ghazwa (Battle) of Bani Quraiza	57 Years	Dhul-Haj 5 AH April 627 AD
Ghazwa (Battle) of Bani Lahyan	57 Years	1 Rabi-ul-Awwal 6 AH 21 July 627 AD
Ghazwa (Battle) of Dhi Qard or Ghaiba	58 Years	Rabi-ul-Akhar 6 AH August 627 AD
Treaty of Hudaibiyya	58 Years	1 Dhi Qa'd 6 AH 13 March 628

		AD
Prohibition of Marriage with non-believers	58 Years	Dhi Qa'd 6 AH March 628 AD
Marriage with Hadrat Habiba, may Allah be pleased with her	58 Years	Dhul-Haj 6 AH April 628 AD
Invitation sent to various rulers to accept Islam	58 Years	1 Muharram 7AH May 628 AD
Ghazwa (Battle) of Khaibar Return of Muslims from Abyssinia. Marriage with Hadrat	58 Years	Muharram 7 AH June 628 AD

Safiyya, may Allah be pleased with her. Ghazwa (Battle) of Wadiyul-Qura and Taim.		
Performance of Umra (Umratul-Qada) Marriage with Hadrat Maimuna, may Allah be pleased with her	59 Years	Dhi Qa'd 7 AH March 629 AD
Hadrat Khalid bin Walid and Hadrat Umar bin Al-'Aas, may Allah be pleased with both, accept Islam	60 Years	Safar 8 AH June 629 AD

Ghazwa of Muta	60 Years	Jamadi-ul-Awwal 8 AH August 629 AD
Ghazwa (Battle) of Mecca and Fall of Mecca	60 Years	10 Ramadan 8 AH 1 January 630 AD
Ghazwa (Battle) of Hunain (or Autas or Hawazan) and Ghazwa (Battle) of Ta'if	60 Years	Shawwal 8 AH January 630 AD
Arrival in Ja'rana Deputation from Hawazan accepts Islam	60 Years	5 Dhi Qa'd 8 AH 24 February 630 AD

Regular establishment of Department of Zakat (Alms) and Sadaqa (Charity), and appointment of administrative officers	60 Years	Muharram, 9 AH April 630 AD
Deputation from Ghadra accepts Islam	60 Years	Safar 9 AH May 630 AD
Deputation from Balli accepts Islam	61 Years	Rabi-ul-Awwal, 9 AH June 630 AD
Ummul-Muminin Hadrat Mariya, may Allah be pleased with her, gave birth to a son, Hadrat	61 Years	Jamadi-ul-Akhar, 9 AH August 630 AD

Ibrahim, may Allah be pleased with him		
Ghazwa (Battle) of Tabuk, the last great battle lead by the Holy Prophet, peace be upon him	61 Years	Rajab, 9 AH October 630 AD
Ordinance of Jizya, tax on non-believers seeking protection from Muslims and exemption from military service in defense of the country they were living in as its	61 Years	Rajab 9 AH October 630 AD

citizens		
Pilgrimage journey of Hadrat Abu Bakr Siddique, may Allah be pleased with him	61 Years	Dhi Qa'd, 9 AH February 631 AD
Hajj (pilgrimage of Ka'ba in Mecca) made Obligatory by Allah Interest is prohibited in Islam	61 Years	
Deputation Tai, Hamadan, Bani Asad and Bani Abbas, all accept Islam	61 Years	

Deputation from Ghuttan accepts Islam	62 Years	Ramadan, 10 AH 631 AD
Departure from Medina for Mecca for Hajjatul- Wida (Farewell Pilgrimage)	62 Years	25 Dhi Qa'd 10 AH 23 February 632 AD
Entry into Mecca for Hajjatul-Wida (Farewell Pilgrimage)	62 Years	4 Dhul-Haj 10 AH 1 March 632 AD
Hajjatul-Wida, departure for 'Arafat, Farewell Sermon Received the last revelation	62 Years	Friday 9 Dhul Hajj 10 AH 6 March 632 AD

from Allah		
Return from Mana, Hajjatul-Wida	62 Years	13 Dhul-Hajj 10 AH 10 March 632 AD
Arrival of deputations from Nakha' Last deputation received by the Holy Prophet, peace be upon him	62 Years	15 Muharram 11 AH 11 April 632 AD
Sarya Usama bin Zaid, may Allah be pleased with him, last successful military mission during the Holy	62 Years	28 Safar 11 AH 24 May 632 AD

Prophet's life		
The Holy Prophet, peace be upon him, falls ill	62 Years	Monday 29 Safar 11 AH 25 May 632 AD
The Holy Prophet, peace be upon him, lead the last Salat four days before his departure from this world	62 Years	Wednesday 8 Rabi-ul-Awwal 11 AH 3 June 632 AD
The Holy Prophet, peace be upon him, offered his last Prayer in congregation in the Mosque lead by Hadrat Abu Bakr, may	63 Years	Monday 12 Rabi-ul-Awwal 11 AH 7 June 632 AD

Allah be pleased with him		
The Holy Prophet, peace be upon him, passed away	63 Years	Inna lillahe wa Inna Elaihe Rajioon
Janaza (funeral) Prayer and burial	63 Years	Wednesday 14 Rabi-ul-Awwal 11 AH 9 June 632 AD

www.ingramcontent.com/pod-product-compliance
Lightning Source LLC
Chambersburg PA
CBHW060918040426

42445CB00011B/687